# ROCK PAINTING FOR BEGINNERS

# ROCK PAINTING

*for* **BEGINNERS**

## SIMPLE STEP-BY-STEP TECHNIQUES

### ADRIANNE SURIAN

TEMESCAL
PRESS

For general information on our other products and services or to obtain technical support, please contact our Customer Care Department within the U.S. at (866) 744-2665, or outside the U.S. at (510) 253-0500.

Temescal Press publishes its books in a variety of electronic and print formats. Some content that appears in print may not be available in electronic books, and vice versa.

TRADEMARKS: Temescal Press and the Temescal Press logo are trademarks or registered trademarks of Callisto Media Inc. and/or its affiliates, in the United States and other countries, and may not be used without written permission. All other trademarks are the property of their respective owners. Temescal Press is not associated with any product or vendor mentioned in this book.

Interior and Cover Designer: Liz Cosgrove
Art Producer: Sara Feinstein
Editor: Salwa Jabado
Production Editor: Andrew Yackira
Photography: © 2019 Evi Abeler, cover, p.ii–iii, v–viii, xii, 1, 4–5, 12–13, 24–25, 36–37, 48–49, 60–61, 72–73, 84–85, 94–95, 106–107, 118–119, 131, 135; Adrianne Surian, p.15–16, 18–19, 21–23, 27–28, 30–31, 33–35, 39–41, 43–44, 46–47, 51–52, 54–55, 57–59, 63–64, 66–68, 70–71, 75–76, 78–79, 81–83, 87–88, 90, 92–93, 97–98, 100–101, 103–105, 109–110, 112–113, 115–117, 121–123, 126–126, 128–129, 132–134; Sara Feinstein, p.130. Prop styling by Albane Sharrard.

ISBN: Print 978-1-64152-196-3
eBook 978-1-64152-197-0

For Lisa, who has painted rocks with me
since the beginning.

For my kids, who love hiding and sharing them.

And for TJ, who has endless patience and support
for all my crazy, messy, colorful ideas.

# CONTENTS

Introduction  ix

## 1 Rock Painting Tips and Tricks  1

Finding and Choosing Stones  2
Tools  3
Step-By-Step Rock Painting  9
All the Colors of the Rainbow  11

## 2 Tape-Resist Painting  13

Gold and Aqua
Geometric Rocks  14
Rainbow Tape-Resist Rocks  17
Shape-Resist Love Rocks  20

## 3 Mixed Media and Decoupage  25

Decoupage Pineapple Rocks  26
Decoupaged and Painted Floral Rocks  29
Mixed-Media Paper Napkin Rocks  32

## 4 Stencils and Stamps  37

Stenciled Natural Rocks  38
Typewriter-Style Stamped-Word Rocks  42
Paint-Stamped Dandelion Rocks  45

## Paint Pens and Markers 49

Latte Love Paint Pen Rock  50

Daisy Garden Paint Pen Rock  53

Marker Doodle Rocks  56

## Dot Painting  61

Dotted Butterfly Rocks  62

Simple Rainbow
Dotted Rock  65

Dotted Fish Rock  69

## Mandalas  73

Classic Dot Mandala  74

Blue Mandala Rock  77

Pink Mandala Rock  80

## Transfers and Temporary Tattoos  85

Floral Rub-On Design Rocks  86

Gold-Painted Rub-On Rocks  89

Gold-Tattooed Natural Rocks  91

## Marbling and Galaxies  95

Marbled Rocks  96

Galaxy Rocks  99

Birds-on-a-Wire Silhouette Rock  102

## Hand-Lettering  107

Love-Arrow Rock  108

Be Yourself Hand-Lettered Rock  111

Paint Happy Lettered Rock  114

## Animals  119

Pets  120

Wild Animals  124

Crowd Favorites  127

## Community  131

Social Groups  132

Hashtags  133

Hiding Your Painted Rocks  134

Get Out There!  134

Index  136

# INTRODUCTION

**I**F YOU FIND YOURSELF with this book in your hands, then we are about to embark on a colorful journey together! Whether you've painted before or you're just learning how, rocks are amazing little canvases. Creating painted rocks is an inexpensive craft and a great rainy day activity, but it's also so much more!

I often paint rocks with a friend, because it's a fun activity you can easily do with others. But even if I am painting on my own, I find a lot of peace with a paintbrush in my hand. Rock painting is for people of every skill level—even for those who might not consider themselves artistic. There are techniques and tips in this book for creating rock art that looks great. We will be covering creative techniques here including tape resist, decoupage, stencils, stamps, dot art, and more. You don't have to be a pro at freehand painting to do this. I've taught countless art classes for beginners, and these rock art projects are designed with my beginner students in mind—every project is broken down into clear steps and is totally achievable.

Each chapter in the book will add to your expertise, and allow you to become a skilled rock artist. We will be building on basic skills as we move from one chapter to the next and increasing in complexity. You can start at the beginning or skip ahead to the projects that inspire you most. If you've painted rocks before and you're just looking for fresh ideas, you can find them here, too!

I am extending a warm welcome to you, whether you're brand-new to this type of art or you already know how fun, relaxing, and rewarding rock painting can be!

# ROCK PAINTING
## TIPS AND TRICKS

**L**ET'S GET ROCKING! In this chapter you will find all of the information you need to get started. You'll learn how to use the tools and paints needed, and what kinds of rocks to seek out. You may find that you already have everything you need to begin painting, but I'll discuss some optional supplies you may want to pick up along the way.

# FINDING AND CHOOSING STONES

Rocks are the primary thing you will need. If you haven't looked for rocks to paint before, there are a few things you should consider. You can find free rocks nearly anywhere you can enjoy nature. On the beach or along a riverbank you can find tumbled stones, which have been washed and worn smooth through time, and they are the best to use for painting.

It's important to note that typically state and national parks have a "leave no trace" policy. That means you should not take rocks, nor should you leave painted ones anywhere you see this posted. Rocks in such protected areas should stay where they are. Likewise, you should get permission before taking rocks from private property (for example, the lovely landscaping stones at your local bank or surrounding your neighbor's garden). Businesses and homeowners spend money for those perfect stones, so keep that in mind, and be sure not to trespass.

If you aren't in an area where free rocks are in abundance, craft and dollar stores have a floral department where you should be able to buy stones to decorate. If that's not an option where you live, contact a landscaping company—you may be able to purchase a small quantity of rocks.

Next, consider what kind of rocks to look for. Much of this will depend on your personal preference, so consider these to be suggestions. The rocks in your area may be entirely different from what I've had the opportunity to paint.

Rocks should be smooth and nonporous, preferably without chips or cracks, if possible. The smaller the rock, the smaller your canvas, so bear that in mind when you're out collecting. I like to use rocks that are approximately 2 to 4 inches long, round or oval shaped, and fairly flat. If you ever skipped stones as a kid, find one that shape, but bigger.

And rocks for painting don't need to be perfect. Sometimes an unusual shape will inspire you, or you may only have oddly shaped rocks available. I've used all shapes and sizes. Also, you don't need to concern yourself with the color of the rock nearly as much as how easily it can be painted. Before painting, my rocks range from white to nearly black. I typically avoid colorful stones, because the minerals in them can give them a rough and bumpy surface.

# TOOLS

The tools for rock painting are few and inexpensive. You can be quickly on your way with a few tubes of acrylic paint, a cup of water, a paintbrush or two, paper towels, and this book to guide you. You may already have many of the tools around your house, and you can do a lot with very little.

## Tools and Materials

**Palette.** Your palette is where you dispense your working paint. It does not have to be fancy! Small 6-well plastic palettes are commonly used and inexpensive, and can usually hold all your working colors. You don't need much paint at a time for the rocks, so you can put a marble-size amount in each well. In a pinch, or if you're painting with friends, you can also use a disposable paper plate as a palette.

**Paper or nonstick craft mat.** You will need to protect your work surface from paint by covering it with kraft paper (available in rolls in craft stores), newspaper, or a nonstick reusable craft mat. Paper can be thrown away after you have painted, and craft mats can be washed and set aside to dry. You may also want to raid your craft bin for scrapbook paper or decorative napkins to create decoupage stones.

**Stylus.** This ball-ended tool is used to create dots. Typically, one stylus will have 2 sizes of ball end: one end will be larger than the other so you can make dots of 2 different sizes. You can substitute other household items for this purpose, such as the heads of pins or toothpicks, but if you find that you really enjoy painting, a stylus or a set of a few different sizes is a small investment.

Palette

Craft mat

Paint pen

Stamp

Stamps

Stylus

Tape

Tape

Inkpad

Paintbrushes

Acrylic paint

Stencil

Punch

Punch

Acrylic paint

Decoupage medium

Paint pens

Brush-tip markers

**Paper towels.** You will want to keep paper towels or reusable rags on hand when you're painting. As you rinse your brushes to change colors, you will need something absorbent to get the excess water out of your brush. A typical project will require 1 to 2 paper towels. You can also wipe up wet paint with a damp paper towel.

**Water.** You will need to rinse your brush after using each color, so having a water cup on hand is essential. It can be as utilitarian as a plastic party cup, or you can buy collapsible silicone water cups designed for fewer spills to keep with your painting supplies.

**Varnish.** Whether you prefer spray-on or brush-on varnish, you will need to seal your rocks with varnish to weatherize them and to prevent them from chipping. In this book, I am recommending a brush-on varnish for its ease of use: Brush-on varnish does not have fumes, and you can apply it at your work-station without getting up to go outside or to another well-ventilated area.

**Decoupage medium.** Decoupage medium comes in many brands and formulas, but you can just pick a basic one. If decoupage medium isn't available in your area, white school glue that dries clear can be substituted. This product will aid in applying paper elements, and will seal inks and markers so that the colors don't bleed when you apply varnish.

**Hair dryer.** A basic hair dryer will speed the drying times of your rocks. It comes in handy when applying base coats or background colors anytime your paint should be dry to the touch. Use it on the cool setting.

**Tape.** Washi tape or masking tape can be applied to your rocks when you have an edge or area you want to protect from paint bleed. I recommend washi tape because it comes in widths as small as ¼ inch, and this smaller tape is perfect for using on small rocks.

**Craft vinyl.** Like tape, craft vinyl will help protect your paint edges from paint bleed. Craft vinyl comes in a sheet with removable paper backing and can be used with craft punches or dies to make shapes.

**Punches and dies.** Punches are handheld cutters that can punch a particular shape (such as a butterfly) in a designated size. Dies, or die cutters as some people say, are used with a die-cutting machine. They serve the same purpose as individual punches, but can make lots of different shapes. Dies can be an expensive investment if you don't already own a die-cutting machine. Dies are far less bulky than punches, but if you're only looking for a few basic shapes, craft punches do the trick and are not as expensive.

**Rub-on decals and temporary tattoos:** Rub-on decals can be found in the scrapbooking section of craft stores and come in many different colors and styles. They make for a striking and simple design when transferred to a rock, which can then be embellished. The same is true for temporary tattoos, which are available in cool metallics and color.

**Stamps and inkpads.** Some projects call for the use of stamps. For these projects, you can use inexpensive mounted rubber stamps, or unmounted stamps in conjunction with a stamp block. At a minimum, I recommend getting a set of rubber ¼-inch letters, which can typically be found for $5 or less. When you are using stamps with ink, I recommend an archival inkpad. This type of ink is permanent, waterproof, and can be used without sealant with no ink bleed.

**Stencils.** Self-adhesive stencils can be used on rocks because they are flexible, and the edges stick to the surface of your rock to prevent paint bleed. Keep the size of your rocks in mind when you purchase stencils; small patterns and designs work best when your rocks are only a few inches in diameter.

## Paint, Paintbrushes, and Pens

**Paint.** The best paint for beginners to use on rocks is acrylic paint. It's a water-based paint, so it cleans up easier than some other types of paint. I recommend that beginners buy premixed shades, so that if you need to touch up any spots, you get a consistent color. You can also mix your own colors, but 2-ounce bottles of ready-to-use acrylic paint are inexpensive, and you will find that you gravitate to certain colors. I recommend buying white, black, red, orange, yellow, green, blue, purple, pink, and brown at a minimum, and select a few bottles of colors you really like. In this book you will find I use lots of aqua and turquoise, so many projects call for those colors.

There is also a project in this book that requires marbling paint, which has a different formula than regular acrylic paints. When you are ready to use this type of paint, turn to page 96 to learn how.

**Paintbrushes.** At a minimum, you will want a ½-inch flat brush, a round brush, and a fine-line brush. I recommend a size 5 round brush, and a 10/0 line brush. You can buy a variety pack that contains all three types of brushes. One size up or down from the recommended size can be substituted. In addition, a stipple brush is a rough brush that you will use when painting galaxy rocks on page 99, or you can substitute an old toothbrush.

**Paint pens.** Paint pens come in a variety of sizes. Typically you will find 0.5 mm fine pens, 1.0 mm standard pens, and 1.5 mm larger size pens. I recommend the 1.0 mm standard size for most projects. You can also get acrylic paint pens or oil-based paint pens. Acrylic pens work best for beginners.

**Brush-tip marker pens.** When you use marker pens for painting rocks, you should use markers that have a soft brush tip. Fine-tipped markers have a hard tip, which can scratch the paint off your rocks when you use them. You can experiment with brush-tip markers with various types of ink including permanent ink, India ink, and water-based ink. When you use markers, whether for drawing or lettering, you will need to seal the ink with decoupage medium before applying varnish.

## STEP-BY-STEP ROCK PAINTING

Now, get your workstation ready with all your tools and supplies you plan to use before you sit down to paint. Be sure you have the brushes you want to use, a cup of water to rinse your brushes as you go, and paper towels. It's also a good idea to work on a nonstick craft mat or disposable paper to protect your work surface. I prefer to use a craft mat, but some crafters like to cover the table with inexpensive wrapping paper. If you need to hunt down household supplies to prep your area, or if space at the table is in short supply, heavy-duty paper plates make an excellent disposable work surface or paint palette.

Make sure the rocks you plan to paint are clean before you begin. Rinse them with water (and clean with a small scrub brush if necessary) and allow them to dry before you begin. Extra paper toweling speeds up this step!

Look at the first stone you plan to paint. Most rocks have a natural "bottom side," where the rock will sit without tipping. Some rocks have chips or cracks, and you can hide these blemishes by simply turning the rock over so the imperfection is on the bottom.

Decide whether you'd like to paint a base color on your rock, or leave your rock natural. Leaving a rock natural makes the process go much more quickly, but painting it a bright base color makes it stand out. I like to choose pastel colors as a base color, because my designs have stronger contrast that way. You may find that for your style, natural is a better way to go. There's no right or wrong. If you use a base color, be sure to apply good coverage (which may take more than one coat of paint), and be sure the paint base is dry before you begin painting your design.

If you feel more comfortable practicing your design first, you can doodle on a sheet of paper, or draw lightly directly on your stone.

Add a small amount of paint to your palette for each color you plan to use in your design. You may prefer to add them one by one if you like to take your time, or if you have a detailed design requiring painted details on top of other painted details. Don't forget: You can always add more paint to your palette, but dried paint is wasted paint, so don't let it sit for too long.

You may find it awkward to hold a stone and paint it at first, if it is small or not flat. In that case, consider using a larger, more stable stone. I hold the stone by its edges with one hand directly on the table and I paint with the other hand, resting my wrist on the table for stability. But with practice, you will find what's most comfortable for you.

When painting, you will be painting the background before the details. For example, if you are painting a tree, you'll want to paint the trunk before adding the leaves. If you're painting a face, you'll be painting it blank before adding eyes, nose, and lips. In this book, we are keeping designs simple, and most won't require layering of paint, but if you're inspired to work on your own, remember that the details come last, and the rock should be dry before adding more layers of paint.

Allow finished painted rocks to dry fully. In most cases, leaving your art overnight is a reasonable amount of time to wait for it to dry. The longer you allow it to dry, the less likely your paint will bleed or smudge when you do the final step, adding varnish. I prefer a paint-on varnish, but that's so I don't have to leave my table and go outdoors to use a spray can. Any rocks that you plan to leave outdoors should be sealed with varnish, or the design will chip off quickly. I also seal indoor rocks, to be sure they last.

TIP: To avoid the old adage, "It's like watching paint dry," you can paint multiple rocks in one session, allowing drying time as you move from one stone to the next. You can also speed drying time by using a hair dryer on a cool setting, or using a fan to circulate more air.

# ALL THE COLORS OF THE RAINBOW

Color choices are practically endless, so how do you decide which colors to use? The key is to pick contrasting colors. You can choose colors that are opposites on the color wheel, or contrast pastels with bolder, brighter colors. I find that a pastel base works wonderfully for the design colors I gravitate to. I like to use pale blues, lavender, pinks, and soft yellows.

Acrylic paint is relatively inexpensive, so I just buy a 2-ounce tube of the color I want. But if you're using a limited set of primary colors, don't be afraid to mix your own additional colors. Use a small paint storage container like a lidded jar if you mix a custom color, and be sure to close it tightly when not in use. Then if you need to touch up or add to your rock design later, you won't need to try to mix that color again. It can be very difficult to match a color you mixed yourself.

# TAPE-RESIST PAINTING

**IF YOU'VE EVER USED PAINTER'S TAPE** to protect an area of a wall or molding you're painting, then you're already familiar with the tape-resist painting technique. The idea is that you can create lines and geometric designs with tape, then paint the rocks, and when you peel off the tape, underneath is the base color of the rock. The tape provides resistance to the paint in the places where you use it. It's a great way to make a vibrant and cheerful pattern, without worrying about exactly what design to paint. Washi tape is a popular craft tape that comes in many narrow widths and decorative designs. It is easy to work with.

# GOLD AND AQUA GEOMETRIC ROCKS

The simple yet elegant geometric designs are easy to paint, and the metallic gold paint really makes them shine. These decorated rocks make for glam decor with their minimalist design.

**Tools**

Smooth rocks 1 to 3 inches in diameter, ½-inch flat brush, washi tape or painter's tape, fine-line brush

**Paints and sealant**

Aqua and gold acrylic paints; brush-on varnish sealant

**Start-to-finish time**

15 minutes prep and painting time; 2 hours drying time

1. **Paint the rock with aqua acrylic paint.** Because you'll be adding tape next, you will need to wait until the paint sets instead of being just dry to the touch. Wait 1 hour to allow the base coat to dry fully, so the base coat doesn't peel off later when you remove the tape.

2. **Apply the tape.** Apply and adjust the tape over half of the rock to create straight lines. Because rocks are rounded, you'll find that the tape may become wrinkled, and this is okay. Just press the tape down well, so there is a firm seal. The more secure the tape is, the less likely paint will bleed under the tape. Paint half of the rock with gold paint.

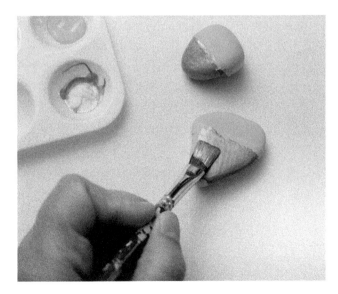

3. **Allow the paint to dry, and then remove the tape.** Once the paint is dry to the touch, add additional coats of paint anywhere it may appear thin. After all of the paint is dry to the touch and you can handle the rock without smudging the paint, gently remove the tape. Working slowly helps to keep the base coat from chipping or peeling. If you find that any

of the aqua paint has come off with the tape, use the fine-line brush to touch up those edges. Once all the paint has dried, use paint-on varnish sealant to protect the painted rock. Even if you don't intend for these painted rocks to be placed outdoors, they can rub or fall against each other and damage the paint. The varnish will ensure your paint stays fresh and doesn't chip over time.

**MAKE IT YOUR OWN:** Color trends are always changing. Try using pale pink and rose gold, or white and silver paints for this project. Each color combination will give this project a totally different look.

# RAINBOW TAPE-RESIST ROCKS

Everybody loves seeing a rainbow—there's something magical in the way they appear after a rainstorm. These rainbow tape-resist painted rocks will be just as magical when someone finds them. Bright colors and stripes or segments make this design very simple yet easy to paint. You can mix up colors in any combination, so if rainbows aren't quite your thing, you can use your favorite color combinations.

**Tools**

Smooth rocks 2 to 6 inches in diameter, ½-inch flat brush, ¼-inch narrow washi tape or painter's tape

**Paints and sealant**

White, bright pink, orange, pale yellow, light green, aqua, and lavender acrylic paints; brush-on varnish sealant

**Start-to-finish time**

20 minutes prep and painting time; 2 hours drying time

1. **Paint the rock with the white acrylic paint.** To create the white lines, start by painting the rock with white acrylic paint. Allow the white base coat to dry fully before you continue. You will need to decide now whether you will paint the whole rock, including the bottom. Painting the bottom gives the rock a more professional look, but it will require a little more time and patience. Depending

   on the type of rock, the brand of paint, and your personal technique, you may need to add additional coats of paint. As soon as the paint on one side is dry to the touch, turn over the rock and paint the other side. The drying process can be shortened by using a fan or a hair dryer on a cool setting. Once the rock is fully painted, wait 1 hour to allow the paint to set, so the base coat doesn't peel off with the tape later. If you begin taping when the paint is just dry to the touch, you risk having it peel off when you remove the tape later.

2. **Plan your design.** Here, I'm using 5 parallel strips of narrow washi tape to separate the 6 colors I'm painting. Apply and adjust the narrow strips as necessary to create uniform straight lines. Press the tape down well, even if you find that covering a rounded stone means that the tape is wrinkled in some areas. You can avoid paint getting

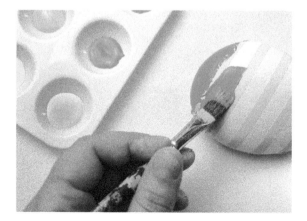

under the wrinkle, or under any part of the tape, by pressing the tape down firmly. You can now begin adding your rainbow colors to the untaped white areas of the rock. To create the rainbow effect, begin with bright pink, moving to orange, pale yellow, light green, aqua, and finally lavender.

3. **Allow the paint to dry, and then remove the tape.** Once the paint is dry to the touch, add additional coats of paint anywhere it may appear thin. After all of the paint is dry to the touch and you can handle the rock without smudging the paint, gently remove the tape. Peeling the tape off slowly helps to keep the base coat from peeling off. If any of the white base coat has chipped in the removal of the tape, you can use a fine-line brush and a little extra white paint to cover those spots. Once all of the paint has dried, use a paint-on varnish sealant to keep your design bright and fresh no matter how many hands it passes through.

MAKE IT YOUR OWN: Don't like vertical stripes? Arrange the tape in different ways to create different effects. Try placing the tape so that it creates a wheel effect, placing the tape diagonally so that it crosses neatly across the center of the rock.

# SHAPE-RESIST LOVE ROCKS

Since you have used straight-edged tape to create designs, you can take the technique a step further! Using craft vinyl, which is a flexible adhesive sheet similar to contact paper, you can punch or cut your own shapes, then remove the paper backing and adhere it to the rock. This reverse–effect design allows you to paint a rock fully, while still leaving an unpainted heart-shaped window to the natural stone beneath.
We will move beyond the straight edges of tape into a heart-shaped edge in this project, moving from tape resist into shape resist. For those of us who love our rocks, it's a fun and fresh way to showcase nature while creating rock art.

| Tools | Paints and sealant | Start-to-finish time |
| --- | --- | --- |
| Smooth rocks 1 to 3 inches in diameter, ½-inch flat brush, fine-line brush, craft vinyl, heart–shaped craft punch or a pair of scissors, stylus dotting tool | Pink, lavender, white, and black acrylic paints; brush-on varnish sealant | 30 minutes prep and painting time; 1 hour drying time |

1. **Punch or cut out hearts from a scrap of craft vinyl.** Peel the paper backing from the vinyl and place the hearts on the rocks. Press the edges down as well as you can to prevent any paint bleed.

2. **Paint the rocks.** Paint the top of each rock with pink or lavender acrylic paint. You may paint right over the vinyl shapes since they will be removed in the next step (see Tip). After the paint becomes dry to the touch, paint the bottom of the rock and add additional coats if necessary. When you are happy with the coat of paint, allow the paint to dry to the touch once more, and carefully remove the heart stickers.

TIP: A tip for the cleanest lines and the least amount of paint bleed: Paint from the center of the heart sticker outward onto the rock. Painting in this direction decreases the chance of paint getting pushed under the heart edge.

3. **Add the details.** You may find when you remove the stickers that you have a few edges that aren't quite perfect. You can camouflage these spots by using a stylus dotting tool or a fine-line paintbrush and adding white dots around the edge of each heart shape. If you're feeling ambitious, you can paint the word "love" on each rock in black with a fine-line brush! (You'll be learning  more about hand-lettering in chapter 10, page 107.) Once all of the paint is dry to the touch, apply a coat of brush-on varnish to protect the paint.

MAKE IT YOUR OWN: Any shape works with this technique. Experiment with different-size craft punches, or try store-bought vinyl shapes or letters.

# 3

# MIXED MEDIA AND DECOUPAGE

**D**ECOUPAGE IS REALLY MY THING. It's the fancy term for gluing paper to surfaces, and if you haven't used this technique before, you just might be hooked after you see what you can do.

When I was little, I could cut and paste at the art table for hours. I've always enjoyed the craft and, of course, you can work it into rock painting so easily! Cut shapes and images from scrapbook paper, printer paper, and even paper napkins, and you can create some great looking art. Decoupage mediums are available under several brand names, and they are formulated to make the decoupage process easy. They are very similar to white school glue in texture, and they brush on white and dry clear with excellent hold.

# DECOUPAGE PINEAPPLE ROCKS

These happy pineapples are such an easy rock project! The hardest part is the careful trimming around the images, so if you can handle scissors, you will rock this design.

### Tools

Smooth rocks 2 to 3 inches in diameter, decoupage medium (if they don't have this tool in a craft store where you live, you can use white school glue), interesting images on paper (I've chosen the watercolor pineapples), scissors, ½-inch flat brush

### Paints and sealant

Lavender, pink, yellow, and light green acrylic paints; brush-on varnish sealant

### Start-to-finish time

20 minutes painting time; 30 minutes drying time

1. **Paint a few rocks in bright, happy colors.** Using lavender, pink, yellow, and light green, paint the rocks all over with acrylic paint. Paint both the top and the bottom, which may require more than one coat of paint. As the paint becomes dry to the touch on one side, turn it over to paint the other side. Continue until you have a full base coat.

2. **Find images to cut out, using magazines, scrapbook paper, or printer paper.** The pineapples I used were stamped and painted to look like watercolors on regular printer paper. You can also search for free clip art online, and size it to match the rocks. Cut carefully around the edges, trying not to leave any white space outside the lines. Coat the back side of the image with decoupage medium or school glue until the edges curl slightly.

3. **Place and seal the images.** Position the images onto the rocks, smoothing out any bubbles. You want to keep the images as smooth as possible. Decoupage medium dries quickly; the paper will remain slightly damp for a few hours. This means that if one of your edges has a wrinkle, or you can't get a bubble out, waiting a few hours might dry the paper enough to flatten

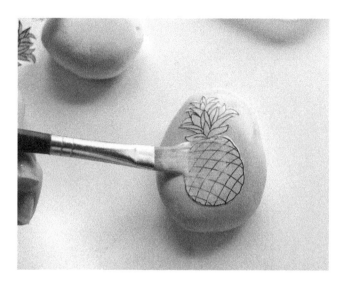

it. You can continue the process by coating the top side of the image with decoupage medium, particularly around the edges. If you have no wrinkles, you can seal the rock with varnish as soon as it's dry to the touch. If you're waiting on a wrinkle to flatten out, wait a few hours or overnight before sealing the image.

**MAKE IT YOUR OWN:** Anything can be printed and decoupaged like this—even photos of pets or people. Thinner paper works best for decoupage, so printing from your computer and cutting an image out works best. If you have a friend with a good sense of humor, imagine the laughs if you make them a highly personalized rock!

# DECOUPAGED AND PAINTED FLORAL ROCKS

Who doesn't love happy florals? These decoupaged rocks in bright colors have been accented with painted dots to give them more detail than the basic shapes made with craft punches.

### Tools

Smooth rocks 2 to 3 inches in diameter, decoupage medium (if they don't have this in a craft store where you live, you can use white school glue), colorful scrapbook paper, craft punches, stylus dotting tool

### Paints and sealant

Orange, pink, yellow and aqua acrylic paints; brush-on varnish sealant

### Start-to-finish time

30 minutes painting time; 30 minutes drying time

1. **Paint a bright base coat on the rocks, and prepare the shapes.** Paint the rocks all over with acrylic paint. Paint both the top and the bottom; this may require more than one coat of paint. As the paint becomes dry to the touch on one side, turn it over to paint the other side. Continue until you have a full base coat. Use circle, flower, and/or vine punches on colorful scrap-book paper so that you can design the rocks.

2. **Start applying shapes.** Arrange the punched shapes to your liking, and apply decoupage medium or school glue to the back side of the paper. As soon as the paper begins to curl slightly, apply it to the rock. Cover the shapes with more decoupage medium, and allow it to dry to the touch (typically 5 to 10 minutes).

3. **Add painted details and seal the rocks.** The simple shapes achieved with craft punches on generic, colored paper look best with a little embellishment. Use the stylus dotting tool in coordinating colors to add rings, flourishes, berries, and more. When the paint is dry to the touch, seal the rocks with varnish.

MAKE IT YOUR OWN: You don't have to just use craft punches for this project. If you have a die-cutting machine, or would like to freehand cut your images, the sky's the limit!

# MIXED-MEDIA PAPER NAPKIN ROCKS

Mixed media is one of my favorite styles for making art rocks, because you can add a little of whatever you want! For this project, we will be starting with a cool paper napkin and using that image as the main design, and then adding a little extra embellishment.

**Tools**

Smooth rocks 2 to 4 inches in diameter, paper napkins with striking designs, stamps and inks for embellishment (optional)

**Paints and sealant**

White or light-colored acrylic paints (they will show through the design); brush-on varnish sealant

**Start-to-finish time**

20 minutes design time; 30 minutes drying time

1. **Raid your party supplies for interesting napkins.** Paint the rocks all over with a white or light-colored acrylic paint. Paint both the top and the bottom; this may require more than one coat of paint. As the paint becomes dry to the touch on one side, turn over the rock to paint the other side. Continue until you have a full base coat. Find an awesome paper napkin and position it on the rock (see Tip).

2. **Use decoupage medium to adhere the napkin to the rock.** Typically I brush the back side of the paper with decoupage medium, but when you're using a thin napkin, it is sometimes harder to position. Lay the image over the rock and paint the top with decoupage medium, letting it soak into the paper and adhere the image to the rock exactly as you placed

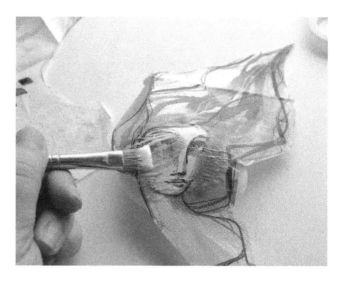

it. This way, you can be sure that your placement is right. If you brush the napkin and misplace it, the thin paper is likely to tear if you attempt to reposition it. You may get small wrinkles as the napkin paper absorbs the medium, but as it dries fully overnight, they will flatten out almost entirely. So in this case, don't worry too much about small bubbles or wrinkles.

TIP: My napkins actually came from a craft store. Napkin decoupage is a fun craft.

3. Let it dry, and add stamps, inks, or paint. Decoupage typically dries pretty quickly, so once it is dry to the touch, you can add embellishments. This is where it becomes "mixed media," so add whatever details you like! Spritz it with metallic inks and use your stamps to add a message. You could also paint dots with metallic paints, add additional pieces of paper, or use a small stencil to get a cool look.

**MAKE IT YOUR OWN:** This is one of those techniques that everyone will put their own spin on; there is no right or wrong way to combine elements. You'll never throw away those last few paper napkins from a party again.

# STENCILS
# AND STAMPS

**S**TENCILS AND STAMPS are easy ways to create images and words when you're first starting out, and you lack either the confidence or the experience to freehand some of the ideas you have in your head. Fortunately, there are so many ways that you can paint great rocks with a few craft tools. Stenciling and stamping may become your new favorite techniques.

# STENCILED NATURAL ROCKS

Leaving these rocks with a natural look rather than first giving them a bright base coat makes this project fast and fun. The blended blue and purple hues and stencils of simple shapes give them a floral and feminine look, but it's easy to change up the colors and make it your own!

### Tools

Smooth rocks 2 to 4 inches in diameter, stick-on stencils (the smaller, the better), small sponge brushes or daubers, paper towels

### Paints and sealant

Lavender, purple, turquoise, and aqua acrylic paints; brush-on varnish sealant

### Start-to-finish time

10 minutes painting time; 30 minutes drying time

1. **Choose small stencils that will stick to the rock.** While you can move the stencils around to compensate for the natural roundness and imperfections on the rocks, if the stencils have a sticky backing, you will end up with much cleaner lines. Use a small sponge brush or dauber—sponge-tipped tools that you can use to add paint—to apply paint onto the front of 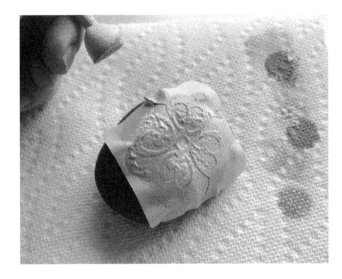 the stencil. When you first dip it into the paint well, it will probably have far too much paint on it. Dabbing the excess off onto a paper towel will give you a reasonable amount of paint to work with. And, as you can see from this photo, I have been random about adding both blues and purples onto the stencil for a two-tone effect (see Note).

2. **Carefully peel off the stencil.** When I removed my stencil, I decided my rock needed more paint. So, I placed a new, smaller, coordinating stencil along an edge, and continued to dab paint onto it. Just be careful at this point: Be sure the first stencil is all the way dry if you plan to overlap any part of the first design, or avoid it completely by placing the stencil in a different place.

NOTE: If you have opted to paint the rock with a base coat, the sticky stencil can remove the paint if it's not dry enough. Before you stick anything onto a painted rock, you should let it dry for a minimum of an hour, and preferably overnight if you want to be sure it comes out perfectly.

3. **Dry and seal the designs.**
   Once the paint is dry to
   the touch, you can use
   brush-on varnish to seal it
   and prevent chipping. Keep
   in mind that the varnish will
   give the rock a "wet look" and
   it will look darker after you
   seal it.

**MAKE IT YOUR OWN:** Different stencils
will give you an entirely different look. If you own a
vinyl-cutting machine, you can use stencils as simple or
as elaborate as you like. Otherwise, a craft punch or a pair
of scissors will allow you to cut shapes in small pieces of
craft vinyl.

# TYPEWRITER-STYLE STAMPED-WORD ROCKS

These rocks are small, but words are mighty! Brighten someone's day with a word of encouragement when they find one of these bright little pebbles. They're easy to paint, and it's fun to express yourself!

**Tools**

Smooth rocks or pebbles about 1 inch in diameter, ½-inch flat brush, ¼-inch letter stamps, archival ink

**Paints and sealant**

Yellow acrylic paint; brush-on varnish sealant

**Start-to-finish time**

20 minutes painting time; 30 minutes drying time

1. **Paint a bright base coat on the rocks.** Paint the pebbles all over with yellow acrylic paint. Paint both the top and the bottom, which may require more than one coat of paint. As your paint becomes dry to the touch on one side, turn it over to paint the other side. Continue until you have a full base coat.

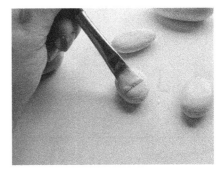

2. **Get the stamps ready.** My set of stamps is a well-loved set of rubber-mounted stamps in a typewriter-style font. You can find vintage sets online, or check the dollar bins at local craft stores. Any font will work if you already have your favorite, but the small size (¼-inch letters) makes a great size for this project (see Tip). The best type of ink to use for these is anything

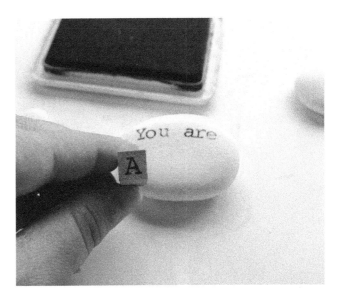

from the scrapbooking section in the store that is labeled "archival" ink. Water-based inks tend to bleed when you seal them. If water-based ink is all you have, you might want to use a test coat of craft glue over the letters once the ink is dry.

3. **Seal the rocks.** This project really is quick and simple. All you need to do now is brush on a coat of varnish to seal the paint and let it dry.

**MAKE IT YOUR OWN:** Have some fun in your office by leaving an inspirational rock on a coworker's desk. A few phrases like "Hang in There!" or "TGIF!" can make just about anyone stop and smile.

**TIP:** If you are using these letters for the first time, try a test run on a sheet of paper to get a feel for how long your word or phrase will be, and if it's going to fit in your rock design. You can check placement of the letters where the stamp contacts the rock, aligning letters based on the position of the previous letter. A little error in alignment is perfectly fine. This project embraces the flaws of stamping letters by hand. As you encounter curves on your rock, roll the stamp over the curve so that all parts of the letter come into contact with the stamp.

# PAINT-STAMPED DANDELION ROCKS

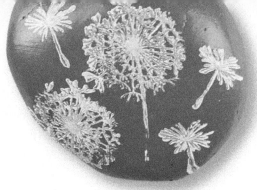

Similar to the stamped-word rocks, you can use other stamps with paint for almost any kind of design! These dandelion puffs are sweet and whimsical, and they're not difficult to apply. When using stamps on rocks, you should do a test or two to see how much ink or paint works best.

### Tools

Smooth rocks 2 to 4 inches in diameter, mounted or unmounted stamps, plastic baggie or a craft mat card-board (optional)

### Paints and sealant

Teal blue and white acrylic paints; brush-on varnish sealant

### Start-to-finish time

10 minutes design time; 30 minutes drying time

1. **Choose the flattest stones you can find.** Stamping on paper is easy, but when you've got something with a curved surface, it can be trickier. I use clear unmounted stamps on a clear acrylic base here to help show you what I'm doing, but any style of stamp will work. Smaller stamps will be easier than larger stamps, but with a little patience, you can use almost any stamp. Paint the rocks all over with  a dark acrylic paint, like the teal I've chosen here. Paint both the top and the bottom, which may require more than one coat of paint. As the paint becomes dry to the touch on one side, turn it over to paint the other side. Continue until you have a full base coat over the entire stone.

2. **Prepare the paint for stamping.** To use a stamp with paint, you'll need a very thin coat of paint. I have spread a bit of white paint around on a plastic baggie to dip the stamp into (see Note). Dip the stamp into the paint, and stamp it a few times to get any excess "blobs" off the stamp.

3. **Stamp away.** Once the stamp is prepped, press it gently against the rock. If you press too hard, you'll get a few of those paint blobs I was referring to. If you examine the photo, you'll see that the stamp is making contact with the rock where you can see the blue lines at the bottom two-thirds of the stamp. To get the top of the "puff," roll the stamp upward slightly until the upper part of the stamp has also made contact. Once the stamping impression is dry, brush on a coat of varnish, and allow the rocks to finish drying.

MAKE IT YOUR OWN: Combine these rocks with the previous project, and use the word "wish." Placed in a decorative bowl, you've got some creative three-dimensional art!

NOTE: I put a piece of cardboard into the baggie to keep it flat while I worked, and also so that I can demonstrate with white paint on a white background. It's an optional step, but it may be helpful if you find yourself getting frustrated with the bag slipping around

# PAINT PENS AND MARKERS

**I**N THIS CHAPTER, we will explore using paint pens and permanent markers. If you're the type of person who doodles in the margins while you're taking notes, or who loves to draw, then this type of rock art might become a fast favorite for you! Paint pens and brush-tip markers come in many brands and in a range of tip widths (fine to fat), and you can find them at craft stores, office supply stores, or online. Paint pens can contain acrylic paint or oil-based paint, but for rock painting, we will be using the acrylic pens. You will also want to opt for a brush-tip marker; ultra-fine-point markers are great for paper, but can scrape the paint right off the rock! Set yourself up for success with a soft tip.

# LATTE LOVE PAINT PEN ROCK

There's something so soothing about a hot mug of coffee, tea, or cocoa! I'm a coffee girl myself, but this comfort design appeals to just about anyone. Give one to your best friend, and let her know you think she's hot stuff!

**Tools**

Smooth rock 2 to 3 inches in diameter, ½-inch flat brush

**Paints and sealants**

Medium-tip (1.2 mm) acrylic paint pens in white, brown, and light blue; white school glue or water-based decoupage medium, brush-on varnish sealant

**Start-to-finish time**

10 minutes painting time; 30 minutes drying time

1. **Shake the markers well, and prime them on scratch paper.** New markers will require priming to saturate the felt tip with the paint inside. Press the marker down a few times, firmly enough for the felt tip to retract into the pen, until you see the paint fill the tip. You'll know it's primed and ready for use when it leaves a dot of paint on the paper. Then, draw the mug. If you don't get the edges

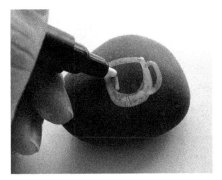

   perfect right away, that's okay! You'll want to go over the design with the marker a couple of times to fill it in, and you can smooth out any edges at that time.

2. **Fill the mug.** Not only will you want to go over the white mug a few times to fill it in, but you'll also want to draw a small line of brown at the top. Wait until the paint dries (this should take 10 minutes or less) before adding new layers of paint. A few steam lines coming from the top will illustrate the toasty cuppa.

3. **Finish and seal the design.** You may want to add a personal detail like a heart on the cup to give it a little personality. Then, when the paint is dry to the touch, seal it with white school glue or a water-based decoupage-type medium. This sealant will dry quickly, and the extra step between the paint and varnish will keep the art from smudging or bleeding when you use a brush-on varnish next to seal and protect the design.

**MAKE IT YOUR OWN:** Special mugs come in every shape, size, and color, so go ahead and get personal! Instead of a white mug, try using your favorite color. Accent it with something special to you like an initial or a star.

# DAISY GARDEN PAINT PEN ROCK

Flowers can make anyone's day brighter, and this design stays fresh forever. This is a great design to place in your garden or to give to a friend on a special day. Daisies represent love, youth, and positivity, and they're universally recognized.

**Tools**

Smooth rock 3 to 5 inches in diameter, ½-inch flat brush

**Paints and sealants**

Fine tip (0.7 mm) acrylic paint pens in white, green, purple, and yellow; white school glue or water-based decoupage medium; brush-on varnish sealant

**Start-to-finish time**

20 minutes painting time; 30 minutes drying time

1. Shake the markers well, and prime them on a piece of paper or paper towel. New markers will require priming to saturate the felt tip with the paint inside. Press the marker down a few times, firmly enough for the felt tip to retract into the pen, until you see the paint fill the tip. You'll know it's primed and ready for use when it leaves a dot of paint on the paper. Then, draw a few white flowers on the rock and fill them in to begin the design.

2. Add details to the garden. Paint in the empty spaces with green leaves and vines and accent them with more flowers. Draw a few tiny purple flowers to add contrast and color. Variety makes gardens beautiful.

3. **Finish and seal the design.** When the paint is dry to the touch, seal it with white school glue or a water-based decoupage-type medium. It will dry quickly, and this extra step between the paint and varnish will keep the art from smudging or bleeding when you use a brush-on varnish next, to seal and protect the design.

MAKE IT YOUR OWN: I kept my flowers off to one side of my rock, because I like the idea that they would still have room to grow. You can, of course, fill your rock completely with flowers or add more colors or varieties!

# MARKER DOODLE ROCKS

If you enjoy doodling, you will have a lot of fun with this project! Brightly painted and colored stones catch the eye, and the nature-themed doodles are simple and sweet. You will want to use brush-tipped markers; fine-tipped markers and pens will often scratch your base coat of paint. Permanent ink, India ink, and archival ink work best. Washable markers can be used too! If you use a water-based or washable marker, you will have a greater challenge when sealing your rocks, but it can be done. The rocks you see pictured here were drawn with water-based ink.

## Tools

Smooth rocks 1 to 2 inches in diameter, ½-inch flat brush, fine-tipped brush markers in blues, oranges, and black

## Paints and sealants

White, coral, and aqua acrylic paint; white school glue or water-based decoupage medium; brush-on varnish sealant

## Start-to-finish time

30 minutes painting and drawing time; 30 minutes drying time

56

1. **Paint a light-colored base coat on small stones.** Paint the stones all over with a white, coral, or light aqua color acrylic paint. The light base coat will make the black marker stand out, and on white rocks, you have more freedom to incorporate different colors. Paint both the top and the bottom, which may require more than one coat of paint. As the paint becomes dry to the touch on one side, turn it over to paint the other side. Continue until you have a full base coat.

2. **Draw.** Once the base coat has dried to the touch, draw feathers, flowers, leaves, vines, or anything that catches your imagination with the fine-tipped marker. You can use these doodles as a starting-off point, and feel free to draw whatever you like!

3. **Finish and seal the design.** It's especially important to seal marker ink with white school glue or a water-based decoupage-type medium before adding varnish. Test a small area for colorfastness; different kinds of marker inks bleed very easily, and some withstand the decoupage medium very well. If you find that the

markers bleed easily, then gently dab them with the flat side of your flat brush. Do not brush across your designs until you know how your marker ink will react. The extra step will prevent ink bleed from the varnish. No matter how well your markers stand up to a water-based sealant like decoupage medium or school glue, varnish is highly likely to blur even the strongest inks, so don't skip this step! Depending on how thick the coat of glue or decoupage medium is, it can take up to 30 minutes to dry. Once it dries clear, add a coat of brush-on varnish to fully seal the rocks and prevent them from chipping.

MAKE IT YOUR OWN: If you have enjoyed using pens and markers, try a design or some lettering using gel pens. Typically, the name-brand gel pens work best, and just like using markers, you will need to seal them with a coat of white school glue or decoupage medium before adding varnish.

# DOT PAINTING

**SO, YOU HAVE SURELY NOTICED BY NOW** that I paint dots quite often in my rock painting designs. I love using my stylus as a dotting tool and for adding the extra embellishment of a few dots. But what else can you do with dots? Lots!

# DOTTED BUTTERFLY ROCKS

This technique using negative space with the stylus is one of my favorites. Negative space is the untouched center of the design with the paint surrounding it, versus the traditional way of painting the subject. Get the look of butterflies without all of the painstaking details of their natural beauty!

## Tools

Smooth rocks 2 to 4 inches in diameter, ½-inch flat brush, dotting stylus, butterfly craft punches or dies, craft vinyl

## Paints and sealant

Coral, orange, teal, blue, and white acrylic paints; brush-on varnish sealant

## Start-to-finish time

20 minutes prep and painting time; 30 minutes drying time

1. **Paint a base coat on several rocks.** This design looks especially cool when you see the rocks as a group, although painting just one is still fun! Paint the rock all over with acrylic paint: Cover both the top and the bottom, which may require more than one coat of paint. As the paint becomes dry to the touch on one side, turn it over to paint the other side. Continue until you have a full base coat.

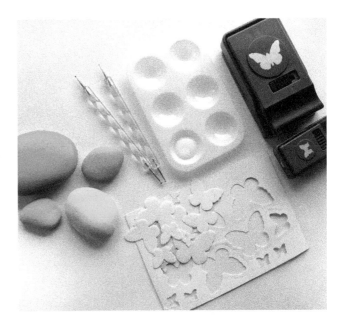

2. **Cut out butterfly shapes from craft vinyl.** This can be done by hand, or with punches or dies. You'll recognize this technique from Shape-Resist Love Rocks (page 20). Remove the adhesive backing from one of the butterfly cutouts (or, 2 or 3 of them!) and stick the butterfly form gently to the rock. It only needs to be adhered firmly enough not to move around; you won't need to stick the vinyl down tightly. Place as many butterfly shapes as you want on each rock.

3. **Don't be shy with the stylus.** Make lots of dots with the stylus around the butterfly shapes. The more dots, the better, really! Especially at the edges of the butterfly shapes, be sure to get LOTS of dots. This will create a more recognizable edge to the design. They can even overlap each other, and they can be large or small. Add dots between butterflies and all over the rock if you want. Then, remove the vinyl piece to reveal the design. When it's dry to the touch (which happens quite quickly with dots), add a coat of brush-on varnish to seal the design and prevent it from chipping.

MAKE IT YOUR OWN: This technique works with all kinds of letters and simple shapes. Try flowers, a short word, or any shape that you think would make a great silhouette!

# SIMPLE RAINBOW DOTTED ROCK

This sweet rainbow is easy to paint, and is a great way to practice using a stylus to get uniform-size dots. Sure to bring a smile to anyone's face, it's also conveniently one of the quickest designs in this book!

**Tools**

Smooth rocks 2 to 3 inches in diameter, ½-inch flat brush, dotting stylus, extra-large dotting stylus or small paint dauber

**Paints and sealant**

Blue, red, orange, yellow, green, aqua, purple, and white acrylic paints; brush-on varnish sealant

**Start-to-finish time**

10 minutes painting time; 30 minutes drying time

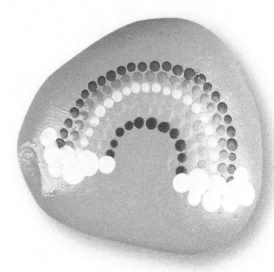

1. **Paint the blue sky base coat.** Paint the rock all over with blue acrylic paint. Paint both the top and the bottom; this may require more than one coat of paint. As the paint becomes dry to the touch on one side, turn it over to paint the other side. Continue until you have a full base coat.

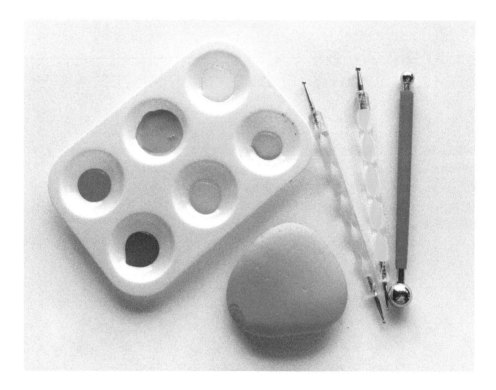

2. **Begin at the bottom of the rainbow, starting with purple and the smallest arch.** This will ensure that there's enough room for all the colors! If you begin at the top and don't make the arch wide or tall enough, you may run out of room. Beginning with a small arch in the center of the rock from the bottom means

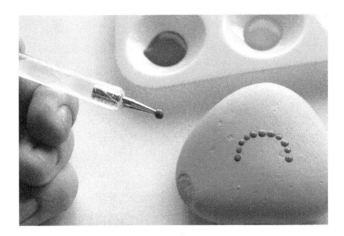

you'll be able to maintain a uniform shape to your rainbow. Space your dots evenly, and do your best to get them a uniform size (see Tip).

**TIP:** Struggling with consistency? The stylus should be dipped in paint often, either for every dot, or every two dots, depending on the steadiness of your hand. You will want to touch the stylus to the rock at the same angle each time you use it. The ball tip of the stylus allows you to hold it in whatever manner feels most comfortable for your hand, but most painters hold the stylus vertically. This lets you get the clearest look around the tip of the stylus to see the size of the dot you paint. Don't dunk the stylus into the paint; just touch it lightly to the surface of the paint in the palette. Too much paint will create dots larger than the stylus, and they may not be entirely round. Too little paint will result in small dots as there is less and less paint on the tip of the stylus. Ultimately, you'll find the most comfortable method of using the stylus after some practice.

3. **Move outward with the stylus, adding the arches of color.** When you have finished the red row at the top, add some clouds to the edges of the rainbow to finish the design. This extra-large stylus is great for overlapping a few white circles as fluffy clouds, but if you don't have a large stylus, a small sponge brush or paint dauber will

work well also. (In a pinch, just freehand it! It's a happy little cloud, so the difficulty level is minimal!) When the paint is dry to the touch, give the rock a coat of brush-on varnish to seal it.

**MAKE IT YOUR OWN:** This is a fun and easy design that you can use on more than just rocks. If you're painting aprons or tote bags or anything with a smooth surface, you can dot your way over the rainbow simply and easily.

# DOTTED FISH ROCK

Mixing colors in a similar palette can give dimension and variety to a simple shape. This fish has dots for scales, and is another easy dot project.

### Tools

Smooth rocks 2 to 3 inches in diameter, ½-inch flat brush, dotting stylus

### Paints and sealant

Purple, light and medium blue, aqua, pink, and white acrylic paints; brush-on varnish sealant

### Start-to-finish time

15 minutes painting time; 30 minutes drying time

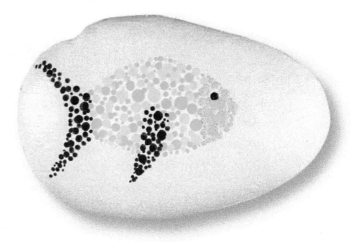

1. **Paint the base coat.** Paint the rock all over with aqua acrylic paint. Paint both the top and the bottom; this may require more than one coat of paint. As the paint becomes dry to the touch on one side, turn the rock over to paint the other side. Continue until you have an even base coat all over the rock.

2. **Create the outline of the fish.** You can freehand this step, or use a stencil to help you get the shape of a fish. Use the larger end of the stylus to create the basic shape, so that you begin with the largest dots. Add an arch and bow to form the top and bottom of the body of the fish, using 2 shades of blue for these dots. They do not

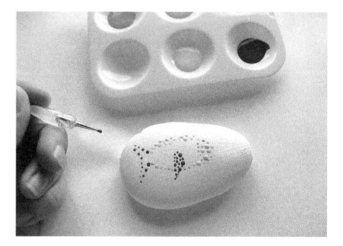

need to be spaced too closely together; you only need a basic shape to begin. Leave a gap on the bottom of the fish where the side fin will cross over the outline. Once you near the head, change the color of the dots to pink, so that the face will stand out from the rest of the body. In the tail area, outline the tail fin with purple dots. Come back to an area close to the center of the fish's body to outline the side fin with purple dots. Finally, block off the area that will be the fish's face.

3. **Add the colorful scales.**
Fine-tune the outline by switching to the smaller end of the stylus and adding dots in the appropriate colors for each area. If you made the fish too thin, this is where you can fatten him up, adjust the shape of the side fin, and round out the facial area. Using purple, give the fish an eye! Then,

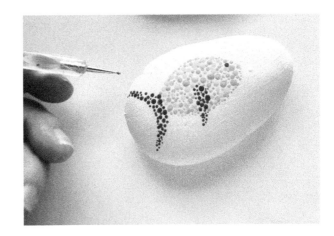

begin adding large dots to the fish's body in the corresponding colors. Using 2 different shades of blue will give your fish more dimension, so in the body area, alternate colors regularly as you fill in the color. Switch to the small end of the stylus, and create small dots between the large dots in the appropriate colors. Try to keep the dots from touching or overlapping. You can also use another size stylus in this step to create additional sizes of dots, if you wish. Tiny dots can be placed along the edges where necessary to give the impression of a smooth line. When you have finished filling in the fish, allow it to dry. Then, when the paint is dry to the touch (which happens quite quickly with dots), add a coat of brush-on varnish to seal the design and prevent it from chipping.

**MAKE IT YOUR OWN:** This design reminds me of a book my children loved when they were younger. You may want to add a few shining scales to your friendly little fish as a bit of nostalgia for anyone who comes across this rock.

# MANDALAS

**M**ANDALAS are ancient painted circular designs from the Far East. They have become really popular painted rock designs because the geometric patterns are considered soothing to paint and view. While there are books that focus entirely on how to paint mandalas, these designs offer a brief introduction for beginners so you can take the idea and run with it. The common theme for mandalas is typically their round shape and their repeating shapes and patterns flowing outward from a center point.

# CLASSIC DOT MANDALA

After coming out of the dotting chapter, it's fitting that we begin with a classic dot mandala. For this design, there are only circles and dots, but true mandalas incorporate many shapes and even floral patterns. For the easiest mandala, we won't worry about other shapes. We will start with simple circles.

### Tools

Smooth, round rocks 3 to 4 inches in diameter, ½-inch flat brush, dotting styluses in various sizes, small paint daubers

### Paints and sealant

Coral, aqua, lavender, yellow, and white acrylic paints; brush-on varnish sealant

### Start-to-finish time

20 minutes painting time; 30 minutes drying time

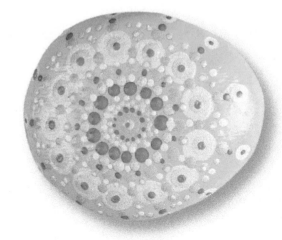

1. **Paint the base coat on the rock, and begin painting dots in the center.**
   Find a rock that is as close to a circular shape as possible, since we will
   be painting a round design. Paint the rock all over with aqua acrylic
   paint. Paint both the top and bottom; this may require more than one
   coat of paint. As the paint becomes dry to the touch on one side, turn
   the rock over to paint the other side. Continue until you have a full base
   coat. Even if the rock is irregular in shape, you can still paint a round
   design. Determine where an entire circle will fit within the narrow area
   of an irregular rock, and begin working in the center of this space. Once

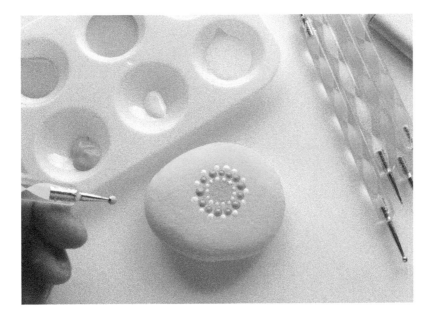

the base coat is dry to the touch, create a large-ish solid circle using a paint dauber as close to the center of the stone as you can. Surround this circle with rows of uniform dots in circles, using whatever colors you like. I started with lavender, and added coral and yellow.

2. **Work outward.** While you can use any size stylus you prefer, you will want to vary your choices, and as you work your way outward, you will need either larger dots and circles, or more of them in each ring you paint. Try to keep the rows evenly spaced and the dots a uniform size. Work in rows of concentric circles for each style of dot, going all the way around the circle.

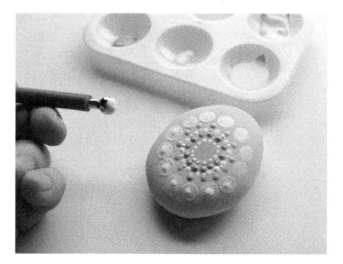

## MAKE IT YOUR OWN:

I don't think I could replicate a specific mandala pattern if I tried. They are always different! Just pick colors that make you feel happy, and enjoy the zen of creating a kaleidoscope of color and design.

# BLUE
# MANDALA ROCK

For this mandala design, we will add some additional shapes to give it a more floral feel.

**Tools**

Smooth, round rocks 3 to 4 inches in diameter, ½-inch flat brush, fine-line brush, dotting styluses in various sizes, small paint daubers

**Paints and sealant**

Purple, lavender, aqua, blue, yellow, coral, and white acrylic paints; brush-on varnish sealant

**Start-to-finish time**

20 minutes painting time; 30 minutes drying time

1. **Paint the base coat on the rock, and begin painting the design in the center.** Paint the rock all over with blue acrylic paint. Paint both the top and the bottom; this may require more than one coat of paint. As the paint becomes dry to the touch on one side, turn the rock over to paint the other side. Continue until you have covered the rock with a full base coat. Once the base

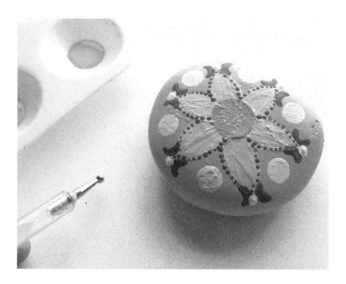

coat is dry to the touch, you can start your mandala. I painted six purple petals with a coral center to begin. The use of bright contrasting colors really helps the center stand out, and the warm hues of the coral color balance the cool blues and purples in this design.

MAKE IT YOUR OWN: Try using shades of all one color, varying tones of purple or blue, for an ombré mandala effect.

2. **Add detail.** Incorporate other colors, shapes, and dots. Work down each petal, adding dots and circles. Add additional shapes, circles, and dots between petals to fill out the round design.

3. **Don't be afraid to overlap.** When you add dots and shapes, don't be reluctant to come back and paint the same area again. As some areas dry, you can add new rows of dots or other shapes on top of dry circles, or on larger dots. When the painted rock is dry to the touch, add a coat of brush-on varnish to seal the design and prevent it from chipping.

# PINK MANDALA ROCK

This design adds stripes and has more of a star shape and feel. It leans heavily on pink and coral, but still incorporates many of my favorite colors to use.

### Tools

Smooth, round rocks 3 to 4 inches in diameter, ½-inch flat brush, fine-line brush, dotting styluses in various sizes, small paint daubers

### Paints and sealant

Coral, aqua, lavender, yellow, and white acrylic paints; brush-on varnish sealant

### Start-to-finish time

20 minutes painting time; 30 minutes drying time

1. **Paint the base coat on the rock, and begin painting in the center.** Paint the rock all over with coral acrylic paint. Paint both the top and the bottom; this may require more than one coat of paint. As the paint becomes dry to the touch on one side, turn the rock over to paint the other side. Continue until you have a full base coat. Once the base coat is dry to the touch, begin in the center with a six-point star shape.

2. **Build outward.**
   Add a second row
   creating another
   six-point star with
   stripes. You can fix
   any areas in the
   middle that you
   aren't happy with as
   soon as the first coat
   of paint is dry.

TIP: You'll find on
occasion that an idea
you wanted to paint
doesn't quite turn out as
you had hoped, which
happened with this
rock design. I ended up
painting something else over the center. That's the beauty
of acrylic paint, which is opaque when dry and covers
previous colors.

3. **Add the details.**
   When you get to
   the edges of the
   rock, you can fill
   in any details that
   come to mind.
   Add dots, lines,
   and other shapes.
   When it's dry to the
   touch, add a coat
   of brush-on varnish
   to seal the design
   and prevent it from
   chipping.

**MAKE IT YOUR OWN:** When you master
the basics of mandalas, it can be very soothing to add more
and more details. Just follow your intuition, and if you don't
like how it turns out, it's only paint! You can paint over
some places, or embellish others to alter the look and feel.

# TRANSFERS AND TEMPORARY TATTOOS

**I**N THIS CHAPTER, we explore how you can add details and great designs to the rocks using something other than paint. Rub-on decals from a scrapbooking source work wonderfully for transferring fine details, and temporary tattoos can even be used to embellish rocks! If you haven't used rub-ons before, they're just what they sound like: Designs that can be transferred to other papers or smooth surfaces (like rocks!) using a transfer stick. If you happen to buy a set that doesn't include a transfer stick, you can use a normal craft stick or a Popsicle stick.

# FLORAL RUB-ON DESIGN ROCKS

This is a fun and easy project that will allow you to transfer premade designs onto the rocks. Choose any designs that appeal to you; the finished rocks will reflect the style you select. One thing to note is that some brands of rub-ons can be slightly sticky. It's best to paint the rocks the day before and allow the paint to fully set overnight in case you encounter a sticky back side to the rub-ons. It can peel the background paint off the rock if it's freshly painted.

### Tools

Smooth rocks 2 to 4 inches in diameter, ½-inch flat brush, sheet of floral rub-on decals, transfer stick

### Paints and sealant

Any light color acrylic paint base (white, pink, light green, or powder blue); brush-on varnish sealant

### Start-to-finish time

10 minutes design time; overnight drying time

1. **Paint a light colored base coat on the rocks.**
   Paint the stones all over with acrylic paint,
   choosing any pastel color you like. The base
   will show through the rub-on design, so
   coordinate the colors with the rub-on designs
   you have chosen. Paint both the top and the
   bottom; this may require more than one coat
   of paint. As the paint becomes dry to the
   touch on one side, turn the rock over to paint
   the other side. Continue until you have a full
   base coat.

2. **Allow the rocks to dry fully.**
   As mentioned previously,
   various brands of rub-ons can
   peel the background paint
   off the rock if the paint is still
   fresh. To cover all brands and
   types, allow the base coat to
   dry overnight.

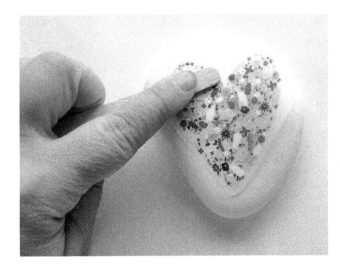

3. **Add the design and seal the rock.** Rub-ons come with a protective plastic backing and are slightly sticky underneath. Trim the design you want to use from the sheet, and remove the backing. The kit should come with a transfer stick to help you get all the details, but if it doesn't, you can use any craft stick. Rub all over the top side of the design (which has a waxy-looking finish), adhering the bottom side to the surface of the rock. Once you've transferred the whole image, peel off the top paper. You can brush it with varnish sealant right away.

MAKE IT YOUR OWN: Rub-ons come in every possible size, color, shape, and theme. Pick a set you love, and you will have a whole set of rocks with matching details.

# GOLD-PAINTED RUB-ON ROCKS

This project builds on the rub-on technique in the previous project. These gold-themed rocks use a combination of simply designed rub-ons and your own painted details. You'll be sure to have a set of unique, one-of-a-kind rocks!

**Tools**

Smooth rocks 2 to 4 inches in diameter, ½-inch flat brush, sheet of inspirational rub-on decals, transfer stick, stylus dotting tool

**Paints and sealant**

White, gold, and turquoise acrylic paints; brush-on varnish sealant

**Start-to-finish time**

20 minutes design time; overnight drying time

1. **Paint a white base coat on the rocks.** Paint the stones all over with acrylic paint. Paint both the top and the bottom; this may require more than one coat of paint. As the paint becomes dry to the touch on one side, turn the rock over to paint the other side. Continue applying paint until you have a full base coat.

2. **Allow the rocks to dry fully before applying the rub-ons.** Let the rocks dry overnight. Once dry, designs will transfer easily to the rocks using the craft stick.

3. **Add additional details and seal the rocks.** I love the gold-on-white effect here and, using the stylus dotting tool, I added a hint of extra color and detail. Using the rub-on designs as the starting point of the design rather than the finished product, you can really get creative. After the rocks completely dry, seal the rocks.

**MAKE IT YOUR OWN:** While I used gold and white here, the set of rub-ons you choose will be what affects your finished design the most. When selecting rub-ons, browse around until you find the design that really speaks to you.

# GOLD-TATTOOED NATURAL ROCKS

Stylish temporary tattoos are a quick and easy way to decorate rocks with distinctive designs. These gold tattoos shine against the natural base rock.

**Tools**

Smooth rocks 2 to 5 inches in diameter, temporary tattoos

**Paints and sealant**

Brush-on varnish sealant

**Start-to-finish time**

5 minutes design time; 10 minutes drying time

1. **Select the tattoos.** I love the gold color of these tattoos, so I selected rocks that would match in size to the tattoos themselves. You can create these rocks with any style tattoo you like. Just as when applying to skin, remove the plastic covering from the design, and position it on the rock.

2. **Apply the tattoo.** Hold a damp sponge or wet paper towel firmly against the paper back side of the tattoo. Most temporary tattoo instructions recommend a 10-second damp application, but I found that when using the tattoos with rocks, it takes slightly more time. Dampen the tattoo for 20 to 30 seconds, and then slide the paper back side off the tattoo.

If any part of the tattoo has wrinkled or shifted, you can gently put it into place with a sponge or a wet finger before the tattoo dries.

3. **Allow the rock to dry, and seal it with varnish.** The tattoo will dry considerably more quickly than paint! It should dry in less than a minute; you can tell if it's dry by the color of the rock. Wet rocks look darker than dry rocks. When all dark spots are dry, seal it with brush-on varnish so that over time it doesn't chip or peel.

**MAKE IT YOUR OWN:** This project is another one that has less to do with your technique, and more to do with your choice of design. Keep contrast in mind when you choose your design: If you like something dark, it's best to paint your rock with a light base coat first.

# MARBLING
## AND GALAXIES

**M**ARBLED, BLENDED, AND GALAXY ROCKS use a combination of colors to create abstract designs. If you find that you don't yet have a steady hand for fine lines, or if you're into more modern and creative painting, you may just get hooked on these techniques!

# MARBLED ROCKS

We are going to stray from traditional acrylic paints with this project and get into marbling or pour paints. The two terms are fairly interchangeable for our purposes, so if you cannot find marbling paints, you can use premixed pour paints or add pour paint medium to your favorite acrylic colors using the instructions on the bottle to change the texture and properties of the paint for this fun technique. Beware: This project is messy! But it's also a lot of fun! I find it to be highly addictive, so be sure you have plenty of rocks and disposable paper on hand before you begin to protect your work surface. You may want to keep going and going once you start!

**Tools**

Smooth rocks 1 to 2 inches in diameter, ½-inch flat brush, stylus or toothpick

**Paints and sealant**

Mint green, turquoise, bright pink, and white marbling paints

**Start-to-finish time**

10 minutes design time; 30 minutes drying time

1. **Apply paint straight from the bottle to the rocks.** For marbling, you will need a minimum of 2 colors. Before you begin, be sure that you have sufficient protection for your surface, like a sheet of kraft paper or a paper plate. Drip or drizzle the paint onto the rock, overlapping colors in some places. The paint will gently run down the sides of the rock, covering the entire visible top area. If you see gaps, you can add more paint. You can ignore any tiny bubble gaps for now; just focus on covering the larger areas of the rock.

2. **Put the stylus or toothpick to work.** Gently drag the stylus or a toothpick (whatever you have on hand) through the paint colors. You are not mixing the

paints together, but rather dragging paint from one area of the rock to another. On different rocks, test out what happens when you drag your tool from one area to another. If you begin in the center and drag the paint outward, it will look like an explosion. If you begin at the edges and drag toward a center point, you can create loops or petals. If you drag paint from one side to the other, you'll get arrows. Use this time to ensure that all the tiny bubble gaps get covered in paint.

3.  **Move the rock to a designated area to dry.** You will get a lot of runoff paint with this project! As soon as you're done designing, move the rock out of the puddle of paint. Marbling paints dry quickly so that you can layer and swirl the paints without all of it running off the rock. If you leave the rock in its runoff paint to dry, you will have a difficult time removing that runoff paint from the painting  surface! Remove the rocks to a separate sheet of paper to finish drying, and discard the paper with the runoff paint. This type of paint will not need a coat of varnish to seal it, unless you plan for the rock to be outside permanently.

TIP: If you take to this technique, check thrift stores or flea markets for old baking racks designed to cool cookies and cakes. Set these up directly over a garbage can to eliminate the mess of runoff paint.

# GALAXY ROCKS

Calling all space lovers! These cosmic designs are fun to paint and give a beautiful, abstract result. Have fun painting constellations, stars, space dust, and gases, or whatever elements of space are most interesting to you.

### Tools

Smooth rocks 1 to 2 inches in diameter, ½-inch flat brush, stipple brush or old toothbrush, stylus

### Paints and sealant

Navy, purple, black, aqua, fuchsia, and white acrylic paints; brush-on varnish sealant

### Start-to-finish time

20 minutes design time; 40 minutes drying time

1. **Paint the base coat on the rock.** Paint the stones all over with navy acrylic paint. Paint both the top and the bottom; this may require more than one coat of paint. As the paint becomes dry to the touch on one side, turn the rock over to paint the other side. Continue until you have a full base coat. Repaint a fresh coat of navy paint on the top, and add in some purple and black in different places while the paint is still wet. Brush over these areas so that instead of solid patches of color, they begin to blend.

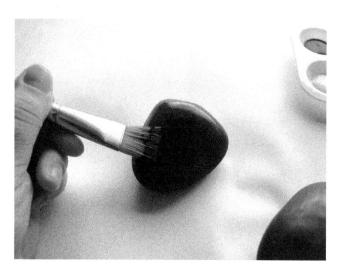

2. **Add color.** This is the first project in this book requiring a stipple brush. A stipple brush is a blunt-edge, rough paintbrush that adds color in a patchy pattern. It is ideal for adding aqua and fuchsia space dust to give the rocks some color.

3. **Add the stars.** Space is really big. There are lots of stars, including some very far away. So we will again use the stipple brush, add white paint to the tip, and add the paint to the rock in a spray. To do this, put your thumb on the bristles of the brush, and run it over the flat surface of the brush. This will spray tiny white dots onto the rock. Do this in a few places so there

aren't any black holes. If you don't have a stipple brush, you can create the same effect with an old toothbrush. You can also add closer, brighter stars using your stylus to make larger dots. Once the design is completely dry, seal it with a coat of brush-on varnish.

**MAKE IT YOUR OWN:** Blue hues indicate clusters of newer cosmic systems, and reds and pinks indicate older systems. There is no right or wrong way to paint these rocks, because the universe is so vast, whatever you paint is sure to resemble one of the wonders out there!

# BIRDS-ON-A-WIRE SILHOUETTE ROCK

Blending paint colors is a little more complex than giving the rocks an allover base coat, but the result can be really impressive, especially when combined with silhouette-style designs like these birds on a wire.

**Tools**

Smooth rocks about 3 inches in diameter, ½-inch flat brush, fine-line brush, stylus (optional)

**Paints and sealant**

Pink, deep purple, black, and white acrylic paints; brush-on varnish sealant

**Start-to-finish time**

20 minutes design time; 30 minutes drying time

1. Paint the top of the rock half pink and half purple. You can choose either color for the bottom of the rock. I chose deep purple, and once it was dry to the touch, I turned to the top of the rock. I painted the bottom half deep purple and the top half a fuchsia-pink. Blending the line isn't difficult; it just takes a bit of patience. Once the paint begins to dry a little,

where it can still be spread but it bleeds onto other colors, paint that half-and-half line gently until you get a smooth blend of the two colors. If you don't get it right the first time (or the second), no worries! The best thing about paint is that you can keep adding a little more until you get it just right. Once you're happy with your blend, allow the rock to dry to the touch.

2. **Paint the silhouette.** Birds are
   simple silhouettes because
   they basically just have a
   body, head, and tail. With a
   fine-line paintbrush, paint
   a horizontal wire and add a
   couple of birds. You can keep
   them simple, facing one direction with no details beyond
   the basic body shape of a
   circle for the head, oval for
   the body and triangle for the

   tail. Or you can do what I did:
   I painted one with a slight side profile, adding a bit of beak
   and a foot. You can get as detailed as you like in this step.

   MAKE IT YOUR OWN: Prefer to paint
   something other than birds? Try a cowboy, a city skyline,
   trees, or whatever you enjoy painting most!

3. **Add the final details.** I used my stylus to add a couple of stars in the sky. Once the design is completely dry, seal it with a coat of brush-on varnish.

# HAND-LETTERING

**H**AND-LETTERING IS A HOT TREND, allowing you to create art out of nothing more than a simple word or phrase. What I like best about painted hand-lettering is that an extra coat of paint or touching up an edge is an easy way to fix mistakes. Plus, everyone loves to find rocks with positive messages!

# LOVE-ARROW ROCK

One simple word can still be artistic and fun! Spread *love* wherever you go when you leave these hand-lettered rocks.

### Tools

Smooth rocks 2 to 3 inches in diameter, ½-inch flat brush, fine-line brush

### Paints and sealant

Yellow, teal, and aqua acrylic paints; brush-on varnish sealant

### Start-to-finish time

20 minutes painting time; 30 minutes drying time

1. **Paint the base coat and begin the word lettering.** Paint the rock all over with yellow acrylic paint. Paint both the top and the bottom; this may require more than one coat of paint. As the paint becomes dry to the touch on one side, turn the rock over and paint the other side. Continue until you have a full base coat. Having a base coat when you're doing hand-lettering is helpful, because you can "erase" mistakes or fill out your letters evenly by touching up the edges with the base color. If the letters aren't perfect at first, you can easily fix them with a little more paint.

2. **Fill in the main details.**
Using the fine-line brush,
even out the letters and
sharpen up the edges, adding
more yellow in places if you
need to. Then, add stripes to
the letters and paint the front
and back ends of the arrow.

3. **Make the final touches, and
seal the rock.** A second color
of blue here really brings
out the striped effect. Finish
filling out the last details,
and when the paint is dry to
the touch, brush on a coat of
varnish to seal the design.

### MAKE IT YOUR OWN:

There are limitless possibilities when
you're making hand-lettered word
art. Mix up the colors, use polka dots,
or get sassy with your message.

# BE YOURSELF
# HAND-LETTERED ROCK

A great message to anyone: be yourself. Mix font types and add flourishes and dots to take this design from plain to perfect!

**Tools**

Smooth rocks 2 to 3 inches in diameter, ½-inch flat brush, fine-line brush

**Paints and sealant**

Aqua and black acrylic paints; brush-on varnish sealant

**Start-to-finish time**

20 minutes painting time; 30 minutes drying time

1. **Paint the base coat and begin the word lettering.** Paint the rock all over with aqua acrylic paint. Paint both the top and the bottom; this may require more than one coat of paint. As the paint becomes dry to the touch on one side, turn the rock over to paint the other side. Continue until you have a full base coat. Having a base coat when you're doing hand-lettering is helpful, because you can "erase" mistakes or fill out your letters evenly by touching up the edges with the base color. When the base coat is dry to the touch, begin the letters.

MAKE IT YOUR OWN: Any inspirational design is a treasure to find! Not feeling "Be Yourself"? Try "Be Inspired" or "Be Artistic." The words you choose will show the love and care you put into painting them.

2. **Fill in the main details.** Using the fine-line brush, fill out the cursive letters. Since "yourself" is the longer word, that's where I started. "Be" is a much shorter word, so I filled it in above "yourself" and added a little flourish to balance out the image.

3. **Make the final touches, and seal the rock.** At the last minute, I added a few large dots under the words, and I touched up any mistakes with aqua paint. As soon as it's all dry to the touch, brush on a coat of varnish to seal the design.

# PAINT HAPPY LETTERED ROCK

This sentiment sums up rock painting for me: Paint happy! This project combines a simple design with hand-lettering for a cheerful look that I just love.

### Tools

Smooth rocks 2 to 3 inches in diameter, ½-inch flat brush, #5 round brush, fine-line brush

### Paints and sealant

Coral, white, and black acrylic paints for the base coat, paint palette, and lettering, plus various colors to dab on the painter's palette; brush-on varnish sealant

### Start-to-finish time

30 minutes painting time; 30 minutes drying time

1. **Paint the base coat.** Paint the rock all over with coral acrylic paint. Paint both the top and the bottom; this may require more than one coat of paint. As the paint becomes dry to the touch on one side, turn the rock over to paint the other side. Continue until you have a full base coat. When the base coat is dry to the touch, move on to adding the details.

2. **Paint the painter's palette.** Using a #5 round brush, paint the palette white. It's a simple shape, but the art lends greater meaning to the message.

3. **Add the message: paint happy!** You now know that you only need to outline the letters in black with the fine-down brush in your first pass. Then, adjust the spacing, the loops, and the shapes of the letters by adding more paint, a little at a time. Don't forget: As before, you can use the white background paint to come back and fix any letters that may have gotten away from you. When you're finished, add tiny dabs of color to the painter's palette to make it look authentic. As soon as all the paint is dry to the touch, brush on a coat of varnish to seal the design.

MAKE IT YOUR OWN: You can change the colors on this rock to be anything you like: try shades of purple, blue, green, and more. Your palette can reflect the colors that make you happy when you paint!

# ANIMALS

**C**ARTOON ANIMALS are my favorite items to paint, and will always be part of my signature style. In this chapter, we will talk less about technique, and instead I will show you examples of some of my favorite animals to paint. You can use these designs as painting inspiration to recreate or simply enjoy!

# PETS

We certainly love our pets, don't we? In this section I'll point out a few ideas for painting cats, dogs, and even goldfish!

### Tools

Smooth rocks 2 to 4 inches in diameter, ½-inch flat brush, #5 round brush, fine-line brush

### Paints and sealant

Yellow, lavender, purple, pink, orange, green, black, and white acrylic paints; brush-on varnish sealant

### Start-to-finish time

15 minutes painting time for each rock; 30 minutes drying time

## FAT CAT

Paint 2 rocks all over with acrylic paint, on the top and bottom, as we have been doing throughout this book. On one rock, paint a yellow fat cat. At first he looks just like a lump, so I used black paint to line the features. When you outline his front legs and give him a facial features, he is clearly a cat!

On the second rock, I painted another classic cat design, an "I walked all over your stuff and left paw prints" image. If you have a cat, you know! When the cat is dry to the touch, seal with the brush-on varnish.

## HAPPY DOG

There are so many breeds of dogs; I just made this one a mutt. Paint a rock all over with acrylic paint, on the top and bottom, as we have been doing throughout this book. Start with a pear-shaped head and distinguish the muzzle by making it a slightly lighter color. Under his head,

I painted a bone, so that I could avoid painting the body. This works just as well! Paint his paws over the bone and give him some long ears and spots. The eyes are just black dots, he has a classic "T" nose, and his pink tongue is hanging out of a smiling mouth. You can get as creative as you want! When the dog is dry to the touch, seal with the brush-on varnish.

## GOLDFISH

The key to drawing a gold-fish bowl is to get that nice rounded shape. Paint a rock all over with acrylic paint, on the top and bottom, as we have been doing throughout this book. If you use a watery background color for the base coat, you will have some wiggle room for painting over any mistakes, and you

don't have to fill the bowl. The fish himself is a simple little guy; you just have to make him at home with a little gravel and perhaps a plant to hide behind. A few bubbles give the bowl a full-of-water look without having to paint in anything highly realistic. When the fish rock is dry to the touch, seal with the brush-on varnish.

**MAKE IT YOUR OWN:** Have you ever tried using your pet as the painting subject? What's special and unique about your companion?

# WILD ANIMALS

It's not just our pets that are adorable animals, but also those favorites from the forest or the zoo rank right up there on the cuteness scale! In this section, I'll paint a fox and an owl.

### Tools

Smooth rocks 2 to 4 inches in diameter, ½-inch flat brush, #5 round brush, fine-line brush

### Paints and sealant

Blue, yellow, orange, turquoise, aqua, black, and white acrylic paints; brush-on varnish sealant

### Start-to-finish time

15 minutes painting time for each rock; 30 minutes drying time

# FOX

Paint a rock all over with acrylic paint, on the top and bottom, as we have been doing throughout this book. The fox face is the toughest to nail down, but if you think of it as a T-shape in orange, then fill out the top of the head and add his ears, you've got most of it! The white under the T-shape fills out

what is sort of a football-shaped head. I basically used the body of the cat, with just a rounded, sitting position, and painted the arms black for contrast. I outlined the major elements with black. The tail is an essential feature too—it's pointy and fluffy—so just paint it orange with some white at the tip. You can just use dots to make his face: one dot at the bottom of the orange T for his nose, and two dots for the eyes, set in the white parts of the face.

## OWL

Paint a rock all over with acrylic paint, on the top and bottom, as we have been doing throughout this book. What makes an owl so cute are those huge eyes, but you have to paint the body to get there. Simply paint an oval body, and add some football-shaped wings in a contrasting color. I gave him

a few belly feathers and little pink feet for perching in a tree. The head is just a circle, and remember, owls have those tufted ears. Then, you'll need two large circles for the eyes, with smaller black pupils, and a cute little triangular beak.

## DON'T FORGET TO PRESERVE THEM!

Once the painted animal rocks are dry, protect them with a coat of brush-on varnish to seal them.

MAKE IT YOUR OWN: The fox and owl are always popular! Some other easy-to-paint wild animals are elephants and peacocks.

# CROWD FAVORITES

These animals are crowd favorites. Not exactly wild, not exactly tame, and in the case of the unicorn, not exactly real! But really fun, and sure to get you compliments.

### Tools

Smooth rocks 2 to 4 inches in diameter, ½-inch flat brush, #5 round brush, fine-line brush

### Paints and sealant

Blue, yellow, orange, turquoise, aqua, black, and white acrylic paints; brush-on varnish sealant

### Start-to-finish time

15 minutes painting time for each rock; 30 minutes drying time

## LLAMA

Paint a rock all over with acrylic paint, on the top and bottom, as we have been doing throughout this book. This happy llama is easy to paint, with an L-shaped body and an oval head. You can define the legs by outlining them, and don't forget to paint his fluffy hair! A little bit of scalloped edge along the neck will create this effect, and you don't have to worry much about facial details. This sleepy-eyed guy has a simple facial expression of contentment.

## SLOTH

Paint a rock all over with acrylic paint, on the top and bottom, as we have been doing throughout this book. The sloth in the tree is a favorite of mine. You can paint him sleeping in a tree with a long oval body and slightly oval head. The facial markings aren't difficult: paint a lighter colored face than the body, and darker smudges around the eyes. This one has left his long legs to dangle, and don't forget the signature long claws.

## UNICORN

Paint a rock all over with acrylic paint, on the top and bottom, as we have been doing throughout this book. Unicorns and horses are a little more advanced, and the shape of their heads and their legs make all the difference. Remember that the hind legs of a horse, pegasus, or unicorn have joints that allow it to walk forward and backward, so by painting the hindquarters more realistically, you'll achieve a convincing character.

MAKE IT YOUR OWN: If you love these ideas and want even more, you can do an Internet search for "free clip art" or "rock painting ideas." I recommend printing out several clip art designs to refer to when trying to get the look you want.

# COMMUNITY

**T**HE ROCK PAINTING movement is really all about community. It's a pay-it-forward, happy feeling to spread joy with small painted rocks around your neighborhood, your city, and beyond. But who found your rock? Did they think it was as awesome as you did? Is anyone else nearby doing it too? How can you find out?

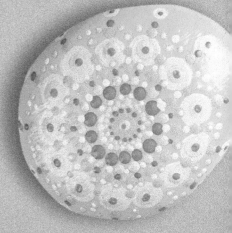

## SOCIAL GROUPS

Fortunately, there are thousands—yes thousands!—of neighborhoods and communities participating in this movement. You may even have a rock painting group near you and not even know it. Most groups connect on Facebook, and may use a special hashtag or other locator. By searching "painted rocks" and the name of your city, state, or province, you might find that there's already a group in your area. For example, I live in Michigan, and on a Facebook search, I found that there are over fifty groups in my state where people can show the rocks they're painting, talk about techniques, share when they have found a happy rock, and more!

If you live in a remote area, you can join a national group, like Paint Happy Rocks, a group I started for people to connect with from wherever they are. If you don't already have a painting buddy (or even if you do) you can join us there to share your designs, ask and answer questions, and just enjoy the hobby. If you're savvy with social media, you could even start a group for your neighborhood.

Why does it matter if there are people in your area who are also painting? Well, have you looked around in your local parks, libraries, or downtown areas? You might be surprised to see someone else's artwork nestled in doorways or windows, near trees and bushes, at special memorial spots. I have even found hidden rocks in my local grocery store! If there are instructions or a hashtag on the bottom, that rock is free for the taking.

So how does it all come together?

1. **There may be a hashtag on the back of your rock, so search for it!** Look on Facebook, Instagram, Twitter, or your favorite social media outlet. You should be able to locate either the group or the individual painter. If you're still not sure how the hashtag works, a hashtag is a search tool that begins

with the pound sign (#) and is followed by a relevant word or phrase. Social media websites know that it's a search if it begins with the hashtag.

2. **Snap a photo!** The happiness is meant to be shared! Post the photo, and use the hashtag on the bottom of the rock in the post that you write. Don't forget to make your post public if you want the artist to know you have found it!

3. **Search and socialize.** Participate in your community group, or search for your personal hashtag every so often. You may see the rocks you have hidden pop up in a search, which is always a great feeling! Even if the finder stays anonymous, you can still feel personal pride over someone enjoying your work.

## HASHTAGS

You can create your own personal hashtag as a painter, or you can use a group hashtag. If you aren't sure what to write on the bottom of your rock, then I invite you to write #PaintHappyRocks and to join the Paint Happy Rocks group on Facebook. No matter where you live, painters from any city, state, or country are welcome to share rock art. It can be something you tried in this book, or something you came up with on your own. Painters of every skill level are welcome, especially beginners!

If your area already has a group, they will have their own hashtag, for example, #PaintedRocksChicago. If that's where you live or paint, join the group and begin writing that hashtag on the back of your rock. If a local or a visiting tourist stumbles across your art, they can search for your group and post a photo of what they found. You would be surprised how far these rocks can travel!

## HIDING YOUR PAINTED ROCKS

I recommend "hiding" your rock in an obvious place. That's the best way to ensure that it gets found! Some places I like to choose are the picnic tables at my local parks, at the base of trees, on windowsills of businesses, the library lobby in a public area, like the announcement board or the drinking fountain, around public fountains, local statues and memorials, and near post office drop-off mailboxes.

If the weather in your area isn't ideal for going on a rock walk to either hide or seek painted rocks, you can leave them on the desks of coworkers, or at your neighbors' doorsteps or near their mailbox. It doesn't matter if you know them or not, a bright and cheerful rock can make anyone's day!

It's important to note that most national parks do not allow rocks to be hidden or taken. If you are in a "leave no trace" park, leave all the beauty of nature unpainted.

## GET OUT THERE!

No matter how much or how little experience you have painting rocks or even painting in general, I encourage you to get out there and share your art. It's a lot of fun to wonder who may have found your rock. Did they keep it? Did they hide it again for someone new to find? Did it inspire them to paint a rock of their own and share it? It's all about keeping the kindness and happy painting going!

# INDEX

## A

Acrylic paint, 5, 8
Animals, 119
    Crowd Favorites, 127—129
    Pets, 120—123
    Wild Animals, 124—126

## B

Be Yourself Hand-Lettered
    Rock, 111—113
Birds-on-a-Wire Silhouette
    Rock, 102—105
Blending, 102—105
Blue Mandala Rock, 77—79
Brush-tip marker pens, 5,
    8—9, 49
    Marker Doodle Rocks,
        56—59

## C

Classic Dot Mandala, 74—76
Colors, 11
Community, 131—134
Craft mats, 3, 4
Craft vinyl, 7

## D

Daisy Garden Paint Pen
    Rock, 53—55
Decoupaged and Painted Floral
    Rocks, 29—31
Decoupage medium, 5, 6, 25
Decoupage Pineapple
    Rocks, 26—28
Dies, 5, 7
Dot painting, 61
    Blue Mandala Rock, 77—79
    Classic Dot Mandala, 74—76
    Dotted Butterfly Rocks,
        62—64
    Dotted Fish Rock, 69—71
    Pink Mandala Rock,
        80—83
    Simple Rainbow Dotted
        Rock, 65—68

## F

Fat Cat, 121
Floral Rub-On Design
    Rocks, 86—88
Fox, 125

## G

Galaxy Rocks, 99—101
Gel pens, 59
Geometric designs, 14—16.
    *See also* Mandalas
Gold and Aqua Geometric
    Rocks, 14—16
Goldfish, 123
Gold-Painted Rub-On
    Rocks, 89—90
Gold-Tattooed Natural
    Rocks, 91—93

## H

Hair dryers, 6
Hand-lettering, 107
    Be Yourself Hand-Lettered
        Rock, 111—113
    Love-Arrow Rock,
        108—110
    Paint Happy Lettered
        Rock, 114—117
Happy Dog, 122
Hashtags, 132—133
Hiding rocks, 134

**I**

Inkpads, 4, 7

**L**

Latte Love Paint Pen Rock, 50—52
"Leave no trace" policies, 2, 134
Lettering. *See* Hand-lettering
Llama, 128
Love-Arrow Rock, 108—110

**M**

Mandalas, 73
　　Blue Mandala Rock, 77—79
　　Classic Dot Mandala, 74—76
　　Pink Mandala Rock, 80—83
Marbled Rocks, 96—98
Marbling paint, 8, 96
Marker Doodle Rocks, 56—59
Markers. *See* Brush-tip
　　marker pens
Masking tape, 6
Materials, 3—7
Mixed-Media Paper Napkin
　　Rocks, 32—35

**N**

National parks, 2, 134
Negative space, 62

**O**

Owl, 126

**P**

Paint, 5, 8, 96
Paintbrushes, 4, 8
Paint Happy Lettered Rock,
　　114—117
Painting, step-by-step, 9—10

Paint pens, 4, 5, 8, 49
　　Daisy Garden Paint Pen
　　　　Rock, 53—55
　　Latte Love Paint Pen
　　　　Rock, 50—52
Paint-Stamped Dandelion
　　Rocks, 45—47
Palettes, 3, 4
Paper towels, 6
Pets, 120—123
Pink Mandala Rock, 80—83
Pour paints, 96
Punches, 5, 7

**R**

Rainbow Tape-Resist Rocks,
　　17—19
Rocks, finding and choosing,
　　2—3
Rub-on decals, 7, 85
　　Floral Rub-On Design
　　　　Rocks, 86—88
　　Gold-Painted Rub-On
　　　　Rocks, 89—90

**S**

Shape-Resist Love Rocks, 20—23
Silhouettes
　　Birds-on-a-Wire Silhouette
　　　　Rock, 102—105
　　Dotted Butterfly Rocks, 62—64
Simple Rainbow Dotted
　　Rock, 65—68
Sloth, 128
Social groups, 132—133
Stamps, 4, 7, 37
　　Paint-Stamped Dandelion
　　　　Rocks, 45—47

Typewriter-Style
　　Stamped-Word
　　　　Rocks, 42—44
State parks, 2, 134
Stenciled Natural Rocks, 38—41
Stencils, 5, 7, 37
Stripes, 17—19
Styluses, 3, 4, 67

**T**

Tape, 4, 6, 13
Tape-resist painting, 13
　　Gold and Aqua Geometric
　　　　Rocks, 14—16
　　Rainbow Tape-Resist
　　　　Rocks, 17—19
　　Shape-Resist Love
　　　　Rocks, 20—23
Temporary tattoos, 7, 85
　　Gold-Tattooed Natural
　　　　Rocks, 91—93
Tools, 3—7
Transfer sticks, 85
Typewriter-Style Stamped-Word
　　Rocks, 42—44

**U**

Unicorn, 129

**V**

Varnish, 6

**W**

Washable markers, 56
Washi tape, 6, 13
Water, 6
Wheel effect, 19
Wild Animals, 124—126

# ACKNOWLEDGMENTS

Thank you, TJ, for keeping every single rock I leave around for you, and for all your support and patience as this book came to life. To Katie Baldermann: Your excitement and love of art renewed mine as well! Thank you for sitting down and painting with me while I was brainstorming ideas. Your whole family is simply amazing.

Lisa Martens: Thank you for the hours we spent in the beginning, when the rock painting addiction first began. The laughs, the experiments, the frustrations, and the rock walks were just what I needed. Your help during that time was a kindness I'll never forget! Our little painters Greyson, Raya, and Roman were a handful at the time, but we embraced the chaos, making great memories!

To the entire Callisto team, Giraud Lorber, Vanessa Putt, Andrew Yackira, Sara Feinstein, Terry Marks, and Ariel Phipps: Thank you for all the hard work behind the scenes to make this book what it is! Special thanks goes out to my editor, Salwa Jabado, and my art director, Liz Cosgrove. Thank you for all of your insights and

suggestions along the way. Our brainstorming sessions and painting experiments challenged me to grow and share even more of my passion with the readers holding this book in their hands.

And finally, to my readers: Thank you for inviting me into your homes, craft rooms, classes, parties, and Pinterest boards. Your support buying my books, visiting my websites, leaving kind comments, and sharing my ideas with your friends has allowed me to stay at home and raise my kids while they were young! I can't even put into words how much it has meant to me (and believe me, it takes a lot to render me speechless)!

You all ROCK! Happy painting!

# ABOUT THE AUTHOR

 **ADRIANNE SURIAN** is a Michigan native who designs craft projects for her community, national brands, retailers, and for her websites, HappyHourProjects.com and PaintHappyRocks.com. She has been writing and crafting since she was a child and enjoys painting with friends and family.